And the Journey Continues

Dr. Jyotsna Wadhwa

Qurate
quratebooks.com

And the Journey Continues
Dr. Jyotsna Wadhwa

Published in 2024

© Published by

Qurate Books Pvt. Ltd.
Goa 403523, India
www.quratebooks.com
Tel: 1800-210-6527, Email: info@quratebooks.com

ISBN: 978-93-58983-24-1

Acknowledgment

This book may seem like a story, but it is based on my personal life experiences in raising my youngest child with my family. This book takes on a psychological perspective of my daughter and any child with special abilities who must someday come out into the world and navigate the people around them.

I would like to thank my husband Mr. Rajesh Wadhwa who has always been my strongest support, or rather, my backbone in helping me build confidence and believe in myself. I would also like to thank my son Parth Wadhwa for guiding me towards the right decisions in life, whenever I feel stuck. And most importantly I would like to thank my lovely daughter Navya Wadhwa for bringing direction and purpose to my otherwise aimless life.

A word of appreciation to my dear friends, my sister-in-law Pallavi Agnihotri for their constant support during the hard times.

A warm thank you to Dr. Alka Sharma who came as a ray of hope amidst the black clouds. While we may not be in touch, we still hope to someday meet you and show you your student and everything she has accomplished.

Finally, I would like to thank the almighty for blessing me and my wonderful family.

About the Author

Dr. Jyotsna Wadhwa (Ph.D Psychology) is a psychologist and special educator by profession. With over 14 years of experience in the field, she has assisted children with special needs and clients with depression, anxiety, dementia, bipolar disorder and other psychological ailments.

Backed by her credentials and her own life experiences, she tirelessly guides parents of specially abled children through their unique circumstances. She is always thankful to God for blessing her daughter and attributes her doctorate degree and academic success to her. She regards her daughter as her life's inspiration and feels blessed with not just her two children but to the many more she meets who need the same care and love.

Introduction

"Behind every young child who believes in himself is a parent who believed first."

- Mathew Jacobson

The life cycle of a parent revolves around their children. Parents embellish their children's lives with opportunity and beautiful experiences just to witness happiness, joy and wonder in their eyes. Parental love is the only kind that is selfless, unconditional and endlessly forgiving.

It is rightly said that "family is the first and foremost institute from where a child learns to walk and succeed within their life circle."

Raising one's child and imparting them with values is perhaps the most important project that any parent will undertake in their lifetimes. Raising happy children is perhaps a more complicated one, especially in today's consumer-driven world where material things sometimes bear more weight than morals and values.

This book is about my personal experiences with parenting and life's challenges along the way.

"Life is a succession of lessons which must be lived to be understood"

- Ralph Waldo Emerson

For many of us, life isn't easy. As children we are usually unaware of the hurdles and challenges that our parents experience in their day-to-day lives. Yet, everyone experiences these challenges. To some these experiences come in the form of mistakes that eventually become our biggest lessons. To others these experiences may serve as lessons and examples to others.

Everyone has their issues and their own ways of dealing with them. A few of us are lucky enough to be born with a silver spoon in lavish homes, with fat bank accounts and a life that at the very least, is financially secure.

Yet, even these folks are not spared by the challenges of life.

We are aware that on its own, raising a child comes with its own ups and downs. One can then recognize that parenting a child with special needs is in itself a different kind of journey with not just its own unique challenges, but also its own set of beautiful rewards.

Maybe, I should say special abilities rather than needs, for as human beings we all come with our own set of needs and require attention in special ways. It is my firm belief that every single child, regardless of their abilities, brings joy, love, and enrichment to their families.

We may have seen a lot of movies that centre on children with special abilities. These films demonstrate their challenges and eventual success. Yet, it is only a movie and one might wonder whether that's truly how it goes or are those stories embellished to tug at the heartstrings of its audience.

I can assure you that the story below is based on my own life experiences. This is the story that my family and I have encountered in our time in the real world.

I believe that we remain unaware of our abilities and strengths until we confront the situations that come along our paths. In being a parent of a special needs child, you are challenged to be even more resourceful and energetic. With time, you will become more powerful and stronger than ever. As we travel through our hardships, we all need a bit of encouragement and motivation, now and then, to get through the hard days.

In my years of experience in working with special needs children and in being the lucky mother of a child with special needs, I have learned that we must accept the child as they come to us, rather than the child we imagine them to be in our thoughts. It's all about raising children as they are, understanding their needs and working in accordance with those needs, rather than projecting our own expectations on to them.

Perhaps, we are lucky to be parents of children with special needs (and I consider myself as such) because they allow us to understand our own potential and learn the valuable lessons of life. There is a universal belief that "children with special needs are not sent to special parents, rather they make their parents special." I couldn't agree more.

Sometimes we are not able to change things or shape them in the ways we want, it is then that we must change ourselves. We must change our thoughts, our beliefs, our perspectives and the way we work. Everyone has their own set of strengths and it is only our own thoughts that lead us to negative thoughts and incorrect assumptions about situations and people.

I believe that we have a solution to every problem and it is only our belief systems that determine how we navigate these situations. The more optimistic we are, the more likely we are to achieve our goals in life.

When a child is born into a family, you'll notice a sense of joyfulness. Parents begin to plan around their child's future hoping to give them the best out of life. In the case of a special needs child, the atmosphere shifts into darkness, a loss of hope, and a general sense of stress and tension all around. It is unfortunate, but it is the bitter truth that is universal to every family who has experienced something like this.

It is at this crucial moment that people need to hear words of hope, encouragement and motivation from their near and dear ones and the people around them, for it is in our societies that we decide whether to accept or reject a person.

Chapter 1

As someone who got married at the early age of 22, my life could have very well turned out the same as that of an ordinary person. During those days, for their own peace of mind, parents were eager to find the right match for their children and have them settle down early. I was no exception, however, since it was a love marriage, I wanted this as well. I got married and lived the happy life of a housewife, taking care of my household, along with other responsibilities that I was happy to do. I had my two kids by the time I was 28 and I was leading a great life.

As they say, "**Man proposes, but God disposes.**"

As a parent and as I'd remarked earlier, I too had planned out our kids' futures and set targets for our family to achieve as the children got older. But destiny had other plans. It was in the year 2004 that everything changed.

However, before revealing this turning point, I would like to tell you a little more about my past. In the year 1998, our son was born and we were all happy, leading a life with him and enjoying parenthood. But ever since I'd become a mother,

I'd always wished to have two kids. I was the only child to my parents and I knew what it felt like not to have any siblings. I really wanted to have a daughter and a son. God had already given me a son whom I loved dearly, but now I wished to have a daughter and my husband did too.

In December of the year 2001, our wish came true and there she was - our beloved daughter "Navya."

On the fateful day of 12th December, 2001 my husband held her in his arms, in tears over catching a glimpse of the tiny girl wrapped in a fresh, white towel.

We were on cloud nine.

We thanked God for completing our family and for granting us our wishes.

Chapter 2

Life was moving smoothly and we were enjoying our time with our kids. However, as they grew older, I observed other children beginning to achieve certain milestones and it was then that I began to sense that there might be a few issues with my youngest child.

But I did not have the courage to discuss any of this with my family.

A few months later, I took her to the paediatrician for a routine check-up. I brought up my worries with the doctor and suggested that everything may not be right with her ears. I was afraid that perhaps, my child had trouble hearing. The doctor, unable to quell my fears, suggested that I get the opinion of an audiologist instead.

So, I took my daughter to the audiologist for an audiogram test. With my fingers crossed and my thoughts in continuous prayer, I awaited the results. The audiologist then informed me that there is indeed a possibility of a hearing issue, but that I would have to investigate further with a BAER test which would provide concrete answers.

That was when I decided to reveal my worries to my family.

As expected, there were several discussions amongst us. Everyone had their own methods of checking on my daughter's hearing. They tried to convince me that there was nothing to worry about and that she was just fine. Somehow, I managed to convince them to see a specialist just to alleviate my doubts, and they finally agreed.

After visiting a few doctors, we finally got an appointment for a hearing test at a renowned hospital in Delhi. In those days, only the BAER test was available for those with suspected hearing issues. Now, the medical field has advanced and we have more accurate tests available.

As we got the reports in our hands, our lives came crashing down. My suspicions were right and my daughter did have a loss of hearing in one ear. It was at that moment that I was convinced that it was all over for us.

We were baffled. I couldn't help but blame myself. Maybe I hadn't taken good enough care of myself during my pregnancy and this was all my fault. It seemed, at that moment, that our lives had come to a standstill. Every day and every night, I would cry uncontrollably, cursing myself for my sins. Everyday I would experience weird, intrusive thoughts that would leave me feeling unstable and off-balance.

It is human psychology. When you experience a problem like this, you tend to think negatively and focus only on the negativity around you.

The audiologist advised us to start her off with speech therapy as it was the right age for her to learn and assess whether verbal or sign language was more preferable. The idea of speech therapy was completely new to us and we found it extremely challenging to find her a good therapist.

And so our hunt began.

At the time I had been running a ladies' boutique which had been doing quite well. I was knocked into my senses and decided to close my business and prioritize my child's wellbeing. I felt too weak and unwilling to handle both at the same time.

As a parent, you want the best for your children. And so my aim was to find the best speech therapist for my child. She would swirl her magic wand and soon my daughter would be talking like a normal child.

Acceptance is a hard pill to swallow, especially when you are aware that things are not going to be perfect in the way you want them to be. I know it is easy to say it, but with my experience I would like to encourage you to acknowledge that your child is different - not better and not worse. Once you can appreciate this, you will be on the path to true acceptance.

I continued my search for the best therapist. During those days we weren't in the habit of searching online, rather we would read signboards, advertisements and rely on word of mouth to get our answers. One day, while walking down the road, I came across the board of a speech therapist near my home. I called and scheduled an appointment.

On the day of the appointment, the three of us (both my kids and I) were at the centre. I used to take my son along with me because after the incident I began to feel quite insecure about him as well and felt like it was only I who could protect them.

It was a small clinic with two rooms. I was asked to wait for a while until finally I could move into the therapist's room. There she was, a smart, young, charismatic lady, Dr. Alka Sharma. My mentor, my daughter's life saver, and her voice.

My vocabulary is unable to capture just how much she means to me, but you can rest assured that my respect for her is infinite.

She asked me about my daughter's history and about my own expectations from therapy and her, as a therapist. I was in tears and requested her to help my daughter. I asked her if she could at least help my daughter develop the ability to ask someone for water through a gesture, at the very least.

As a mother, I was unable to understand my daughter's emotions and needs, so you can only imagine how hard it would be for others to understand her. As we say, no one understands a child like their mother. At the time, all we could do was guess what she wanted or needed from us.

The response I got was enlightening. It changed my entire perspective, moving forward. Dr. Sharma said, "She is just as normal as we are. It is just you as a parent who needs to acknowledge her needs and receive therapy for yourself before her."

That single statement turned a light on in my head. Yes, this was the situation, there was no doubt about it, but now what? Rather than cry about it, we need to find a solution to this crisis and start working on it. I suddenly felt a ray of hope within me. I just needed to focus on it with courage and strength.

We are all aware that we cannot change our past and that we need to focus on our present, lest we ruin the beautiful future that stands before us with open arms.

My therapist informed me that the path ahead would be rough and require a lot of hard work, but she also assured me that nothing is impossible when we have the drive to do it. I promised myself then that I would not stop and I would do whatever I needed to to ensure that my child's life was as normal as anyone else's.

As Martin Luther King Jr. says:

"If you can't fly, then run. If you cannot run, then walk. If you cannot walk, then crawl. But, whatever you do, you have to keep moving."

And so, my friends, whatever crisis you may currently be experiencing, or whatever problems you currently face, remember that one must keep moving until they achieve their goals. For me, my aim was to help my child believe in herself and to help her move forward no matter what circumstances she experiences in her life.

Chapter 3

At this point, you might think this is a story about a mother's struggle in raising her child. My dear friends, while there is no doubt to my struggle and that of my family, it is our little one who would eventually experience the hardships that awaited her. The struggle of learning speech, developing self-expression, and interacting with people who weren't always the kindest. Above all else, she had to find new ways to boost her own psychological and emotional wellbeing.

Things are slowly progressing in our system, but for individuals with special needs acceptance and inclusion are challenges that are yet to be overcome. As a psychologist, I have observed many kids who feel left out and alone in the world owing to their differences and perceived weaknesses.

In one particular instance, I came across a little, 10-year-old boy who lived in my neighbourhood. The boy would go to the community garden everyday, but always sat alone in a corner while he watched the other kids play. I used to make sure to acknowledge him on my daily walks through the garden. In the beginning I assumed that perhaps he had had a fight with his friends. I thought things would resolve on their own (as they often do) and he would soon join them again. However, as the days passed, I noticed that he was still all alone in his corner, observing the people around him.

I decided to investigate this myself and see if I could help resolve whatever issues he may have had with his friends. To my surprise and shock, he revealed that no one played with him as he was not as bright as the other kids.

He was not as smart as the other kids. They understood things quickly while he took his time to learn the rules of the game and as a result, was prone to making mistakes. "Even in school, no one wants to sit with me or play with me because I am a moron," he informed me. Now one can imagine how this may affect a child's mental wellbeing.

As humans, we feel sorry for the specially abled. We used words like "bechara", "poor fellow" while referring to them, but how many of us actually sit with them and listen to their feelings, thoughts and emotions? Not many.

It is usually only the family, or often just the mother who can sense their emotions, but even they aren't always able to provide solutions or validate their feelings. They also have their own moments of helplessness.

There is nothing more heartbreaking when your own people aren't able to support you.

We fail to acknowledge that we share the same feelings and the same emotions. It is undeniable that we have different ways of expressing them, but we must be assured that deep down, we are not all that different from each other.

Here is yet another issue I've encountered in my 14 years as a psychologist. There are some parents who spend exorbitant amounts of money on therapy and specialists, but refuse to actually partake in these sessions. They rely entirely on the therapist for progress and in turn take back a sense of dissatisfaction for the centre while continuing on their quest to find the next doctor.

One of the best things a parent can do is accept the situation they have at hand. A parent's acceptance can go a long way in improving the outcome.

The first lesson I learned from my therapist was that she is a facilitator, a guide. As we all know, therapy sessions last for 45 minutes, but for the remaining 23 hours and 15 minutes, the child is with their family. In the early years, children look up to their family for support and learn from them far more quickly than from anyone else. By "family," I mean the father, mother, grandparents, and siblings. It's not just the child coming for therapy who needs to learn—it's a team effort between the whole family and the therapist.

There is no single set of rules that all parents can follow because every child has different needs, and the way they learn is different too. What I want to emphasize is that we, as parents, need to understand the unique ways our child learns in order to help them become self-sufficient for the rest of their lives.

I understand that, as parents, it can sometimes be difficult to handle these situations, especially with other pressures from home or work. But we must remember that these tiny hands need our support to stand up and eventually walk on their own. Some children might need that support for a longer time. This applies to all parents across the world, but children with special abilities need even more hand-holding in their early years.

In my career, I have mostly seen mothers taking the lead in learning alongside their children. However, it's high time both parents participate equally in their child's learning journey.

While times are changing, more active involvement from both parents can be a great source of encouragement for the child.

Our journey with therapy began with an introduction to colors, and the first color was "black." As a family, we made it a point to wear black every day so she could see the color as often as possible. At that time, we believed she might be a visual learner since her auditory skills were not fully developed or accessible to us.

After a few days, she spoke her first word: "black." Then came "papa," "mumma," and "pani," and her vocabulary began to grow. What was surprising—and a bit disheartening—was that we had initially been misinformed that she couldn't benefit from a hearing aid because one ear was fine while the other had severe hearing loss, as observed in her reports.

As time went on, we were more than satisfied with her progress. For us, as parents, the joy was immeasurable. A child who once couldn't utter a single word was now able to speak, if only a little, and at least express her basic needs.

However, my therapist sensed there might be more to her learning challenges and urged us to consult a neurologist for further investigation.

As concerned parents, we took her to a specialist who recommended another BAER test and an MRI of her brain. The tests confirmed she had severe hearing loss in one ear and profound hearing loss in the other. She was advised to use hearing aids to improve her performance, which gave us some relief.

But fate had another surprise in store for us—more of a shock, really. Her MRI revealed metal patches in the white matter of her brain, which had also affected her cognitive abilities.

Now, the label on her was "a child with hearing loss and intellectual disabilities." I mention the label because that's how our kids are referred to, which is yet another unfortunate reality of life. It was another heartbreak for us that left us in absolute shock. However, this time, I had my extended family and my therapist to motivate me and help me keep moving forward. I also made an important promise to myself: I wouldn't stray from my path, and I would keep going no matter what.

As a mother, I continued visiting different doctors, hoping to hear that the reports were wrong and that she would be okay. These thoughts reflected that I hadn't fully accepted reality just yet. In my mind, I was still wrestling with the idea of "normal" versus "disabled" (I hesitate to use that word, but it's the truth). I think it's normal for parents to feel this way.

During this phase, I consulted a well-known neurologist in Delhi (I won't reveal his name). He took her reports, looked at her, and said, "She's a gone case." Yes, those were his exact words—harsh words from a man of learning. He also informed us that if she was in a regular school, we should transfer her to a special school. If we didn't he said she would be thrown out by Grade 2.

I was in tears as I meekly took the file, thanked him and left his office with my family. That was the last day we visited a specialist.

As a family, we decided that no matter what challenges lay ahead, we were ready to face them. We would not let our hope break.

And through it all, there she was, wiping my tears and hugging me - a pure soul, blissfully unaware, with a smile on her face.

Chapter 4

As we could see her advancing and improving her linguistic abilities, under the guidance of our therapist, we got her admitted into a nearby school to help her develop her social skills and cognitive capacity.

It was hard for her to adjust in an environment where everyone could speak and express themselves clearly. She was quiet and kept to herself, sometimes afraid of going to school. The kids would often touch her hearing aids and ask her what they were, but she was unable to explain herself. She was hesitant to participate in group interactions, but she would excel when it came to some individual activities like dancing or art.

As I mentioned in the beginning, our mentor/ therapist asked me to fill out a form for her in my son's school in Delhi. It was a well-renowned school and during those days they used to have an entrance exam for KG. Even though she was already in KG at the time, her therapist asked me to fill out the form again and repeat her classes. We didn't have the courage to say no, but there was a lingering fear at the back of my mind that she would not be able to clear her entrance and that we would have to admit her into a special school. I even set out to make a few enquiries at these schools as a backup plan.

However, I was wrong. My daughter cleared her entrance exams with merit and got admission into one of the best schools in town. That was the level of trust her therapist and her father had in her and it was at that time that I began to have faith in her too.

Day by day she began showing improvement in not just her language but also her level of confidence. I am so glad for the great teachers in her life who believed in her and helped her in both small and big ways.

Chapter 5

Days turned into years, and she was now in Grade 5. A new set of hurdles and challenges awaited her. In the junior years, children are generally pure-hearted and open, unafraid to make friends and socialize. But my daughter had always been quiet and shy—more accurately, she was underconfident. By now, she had begun to sense that there were areas where she struggled more than her peers, particularly in speech, intellectual abilities, and hearing.

She often came to me, saying that other children would touch her hearing aids and ask, "What is this?" She even asked to cut her hair short, hoping to hide the aids from others. Whenever we went to a public place, she would let her hair down, trying to conceal the hearing aids from view.

I remember visiting a shop with her once, and an elderly lady, noticing her hearing aids, asked in surprise, "Oh, what is she wearing? Is it just for fun?" followed by a string of other odd questions. I was already exhausted from constantly explaining her situation to people, and I often wondered—if it was this draining to me, how much more must it have affected

The gestures, the odd mannerisms, the curious looks, and the intrusive questions—sometimes they were so extreme that it made me feel as though it was a sin for her to have been born this way.

We are living in the 21st century, a time of heightened awareness, yet sensitivity toward others still feels hollow. When we talk about awareness for people with special abilities, it's still a sad reality—people offer them sympathy but fail to understand that what they really need is empathy, support, and inclusion in society, not pity. We spend hours teaching our children with special needs how to interact with the world around them, instead of teaching ourselves how to interact with them in ways that make them feel comfortable and accepted.

It's often only the immediate family that understands them to some extent, while others use their energy to label them with special titles. Helping people truly understand these children is one of the hardest challenges I've experienced.

Having a child with special needs teaches you a level of compassion, love, and patience you never knew existed within you. What they need most is genuine friendship—a friendship that embraces them fully and makes them feel included as a natural part of the world around them.

Chapter 6

I remember when she was in 6th grade. One day, I asked her to share her daily routine of class. As she explained, using her limited vocabulary (since, even today, she struggles with certain grammatical gaps), she told me how she would finish her lunch all alone in class and then walk through the school corridor, watching the other children play and talk to each other.

To everyone's surprise, this had been her routine for 2-3 years—until 9th grade, when she met a few friends who also faced cognitive or other related challenges. They understood each other in ways the rest of the class never could. The other students were simply peers who attended class with them but were never really part of their lives.

Earlier, she expressed that no one plays or talks with her, and if she had been a "normal" child, she would have been included in a group. I believe this feeling isn't hers alone, but one shared by many children like her. Even now, whenever she gets hurt by someone or feels low in certain situations, she often says, "You're all fine, so why did this happen to me? Why did God do this to me?"

Although we always try to motivate her as psychologists, as a mother, I can only imagine how painful it must be to keep fighting these battles since childhood. These are just a few of the incidents she's shared with us. I believe there are many other things she faces daily but either cannot express or chooses not to, perhaps because, as parents, we tend to preach rather than understand. But it does us good to remember that sometimes, we don't need someone to preach to us; we just need someone to listen.

We're fortunate that she is able to express herself, but what about those who can't? What about the ones who struggle in silence, unable to communicate their pain? I believe that expressing oneself is never easy, and it becomes even more difficult when life brings with it additional challenges.

The hardest part of being a parent is knowing you can't always fix your child's problems. It can lead to a lot of resentment and frustration when you're unable to help them or fulfil their deep longing to be included in the world.

Chapter 7

As we enter adolescence, our bodies undergo numerous physical, emotional, and psychological changes. We all want to look good and receive compliments from our peers as we begin to feel attracted to the opposite gender. But for those with special abilities, it's often a heartbreaking experience, as acceptance in this regard is rare. Very few people are willing to choose or accept them as friends, let alone life partners.

Though she grew close to a few guys, within a day or two, they would find some excuse to leave. Unfortunately, these discussions are often not welcomed by some parents, leaving the child to bottle up their emotions. This isolation can lead to depression, anxiety, and other mental health struggles.

Telling her why she shouldn't get involved with anyone is a difficult thing to explain. On one hand, we tell her she is an equal, that there's nothing wrong with her. But on the other hand, we're asking her and others like her to stay away from people considered "perfect," whose senses function flawlessly, as if the issue lies with her. Are we really telling them that they should only seek someone like themselves so two halves can make a whole? Is that the message we're giving them?

At times, when she feels disheartened, she asks us, "Why did you place me in a so-called 'normal' society? Why didn't you send me to a special school, where at least I would have been included in daily conversations and share in their laughter and sadness? Where I would have had friends to share secrets with, where I would have felt wanted and included. At least there, I wouldn't have been judged by my disability, and people wouldn't hesitate to befriend me."

There are so many emotions they carry within, but they often don't know how to express them—or we don't take the time to understand them, as they feel. And they're not wrong. We haven't always offered them that hand which says, "Hold me, I'm here to listen."

As parents, we often have no answers to these questions and feel helpless because we can't ask everyone to include her. Over the years, I've met many parents facing the same struggles we did. Each had their own set of circumstances and challenges, and their own ways of coping. But most had to fight hard to find a sense of balance. Some felt like giving up, others changed their approach, and some are still fighting to find solutions.

Children like her—and others with similar experiences—understand far more than we give them credit for. Expressing their emotions may be a little more challenging than it is for you or me, but they feel just as deeply. This isn't just about her—it's about all children who need a little extra help.

I think parents of specially abled children can understand the point I'm trying to make here. We are not asking for mercy or pity, rather I am simply presenting a psychological perspective on children with special needs.

I would be more than happy if I could change the mindsets or perspectives of just a few people through my writing. It really does make a difference to the children as well as their parents, when others make an effort to listen and be inclusive.

Even now, while I write this, I can sense the emotions and the internal turmoil my family and I have experienced while trying to raise our daughter.

When I used to take her to therapy, I remember her therapist telling me to focus on helping her stand on her own two feet professionally rather than worrying about her marriage. And so we have helped instil in her the belief that she deserves to be accepted by everyone, especially her life partner, exactly the way she is.

On this note, I would like to add that everyone has abilities. It is simply our own patience and hard work that can help them transform into an independent individual.

Chapter 8

There are certain myths that many of us often hear and believe. One common myth is that a person's disability defines them entirely. In reality, a disability is just one aspect of a person's identity. Every individual has diverse interests, personalities, and talents and should never be defined solely by their disabilities.

Another common belief is that individuals with disabilities are dependent on others for life. In reality, they can lead successful, independent lives if given the right guidance and accommodations, becoming just as self-sufficient as anyone else. It's encouraging to see that many large corporations are now offering opportunities for people with disabilities to join their workforce and prove their competence.

It is not their capabilities that limit their performance but rather the lack of a system that's designed to meet their unique needs. With the right environment and the right opportunities, they can excel beyond measure.

Chapter 9

She is currently in her fourth year of a Bachelor of Fine Arts (BFA) program at a prestigious college and is thriving academically. She navigates public transport on her own and manages her responsibilities with remarkable efficiency—sometimes even better than some of our family members. Yet, her struggle for acceptance among her peers persists. Despite her accomplishments, social inclusion remains a challenge. She still often eats lunch alone, as no one thinks to invite her, and when she does join, no one asks about her well-being, her interests, or her preferences.

But over time, she has found strength in this solitude. Rather than feeling defeated, she has learned to embrace her independence and enjoy her own company. It's a quiet resilience that speaks volumes about her spirit.

I believe every child is unique with their own special abilities. What they need is guidance to channel their thoughts, an unwavering belief in themselves, and our support to keep their hopes high as they strive to achieve their goals.

Sometimes, I find myself wishing I could meet the specialist who once told me that she would never be able to study beyond grade two and show them how far she has come. While she chose practical subjects after 9th grade, I want to emphasize to specialists everywhere that it's important to enlighten parents about their child's situation. However, we can choose our words carefully to motivate families rather than leave them feeling dejected and without hope about their future.

Yes, navigating these challenges requires training and expert guidance, and it's crucial to be firm during the training process. My experience over the years has shown me that parents often end up in vulnerable, difficult positions. The financial burden of various therapies, the emotional toll of setbacks, and concerns about their child's future can weigh heavily on their mental and physical health. If we, as specialists, can offer them a shoulder of support, it could empower them to face their challenges with greater courage and confidence.

Trust the process and enjoy the journey with your children.

It's undeniable that we have worked hard with her, but it was her zeal to learn and create a beautiful life that has brought her to this point. She stands proud, declaring, "**I am ABLE** to do everything that you and I can do." After all, nothing is impossible; the very word itself says, "**I'm POSSIBLE**."

She has travelled miles and grown tremendously over the years. And with her, we have grown too. We've come a long way as a family and...

our journey still continues...

"Life is a journey that must be travelled no matter how bad the roads and accommodations"

- By Oliver Goldsmith